FIREARMS ACQUISITION AND DISPOSITION RECORD BOOK

SKYHORSE PUBLISHING

Skyhorse Publishing books may be purchased in bulk at special discounts for sales promotion, corporate gifts, fund-raising, or educational purposes. Special editions can also be created to specifications. For details, contact the Special Sales Department, Skyhorse Publishing, 307 West 36th Street, 11th Floor, New York, NY 10018 or info@skyhorsepublishing.com.

Skyhorse® and Skyhorse Publishing® are registered trademarks of Skyhorse Publishing, Inc.®, a Delaware corporation.

Visit our website at www.skyhorsepublishing.com.

10 9 8 7 6

Library of Congress Cataloging-in-Publication Data is available on file.

ISBN: 978-1-62873-685-4

Printed in China

FIREARMS ACQUISITION AND DISPOSITION RECORD BOOK

Record Book #_____

Period covered: From _____ to _____

Name/Business:_____

Street Address: _____

City, State, ZIP: _____

License No: _____

Phone: _____

Email: _____

The following is excerpted from the Code of Federal Regulations, which can be found online at www.ecfr.gov:

TITLE 27: ALCOHOL, TOBACCO, AND FIREARMS

§478.125   Record of receipt and disposition.

(e) *Firearms receipt and disposition by dealers.* Except as provided in §478.124a with respect to alternate records for the receipt and disposition of firearms by dealers, each licensed dealer shall enter into a record each receipt and disposition of firearms. In addition, before commencing or continuing a firearms business, each licensed dealer shall inventory the firearms possessed for such business and shall record same in the record required by this paragraph. The record required by this paragraph shall be maintained in bound form under the format prescribed below. The purchase or other acquisition of a firearm shall, except as provided in paragraph (g) of this section, be recorded not later than the close of the next business day following the date of such purchase or acquisition. The record shall show the date of receipt, the name and address or the name and license number of the person from whom received, the name of the manufacturer and importer (if any), the model, serial number, type, and the caliber or gauge of the firearm. The sale or other disposition of a firearm shall be recorded by the licensed dealer not later than 7 days following the date of such transaction. When such disposition is made to a nonlicensee, the firearms transaction record, Form 4473, obtained by the licensed dealer shall be retained, until the transaction is recorded, separate from the licensee's Form 4473 file and be readily available for inspection. When such disposition is made to a licensee, the commercial record of the transaction shall be retained, until the transaction is recorded, separate from other commercial documents maintained by the licensed dealer, and be readily available for inspection. The record shall show the date of the sale or other disposition of each firearm, the name and address of the person to whom the firearm is transferred, or the name and license number of the person to whom transferred if such person is a licensee, or the firearms transaction record, Form 4473, serial number if the licensed dealer transferring the firearm serially numbers the Forms 4473 and files them numerically. The format required for the record of receipt and disposition of firearms is as follows:

FIREARMS ACQUISITION AND DISPOSITION RECORD

Description of firearm					Receipt		Disposition		
Manufacturer and/or Importer	Model	Serial No.	Type	Caliber or gauge	Date	Name and address or name and license No.	Date	Name	Address or license No. if licensee, or Form 4473 Serial No. if Forms 4473 filed numerically

NOTES

ACQUISITION

	DESCRIPTION OF FIREARM					RECEIPT			
	MANUFACTURER AND/ OR IMPORTER	MODEL	SERIAL NO.	TYPE	CALIBER OR GAUGE	DATE	TAG (optional)	COST (optional)	NAME AND ADDRESS OR NAME AND LICENSE NO.
1									
2									
3									
4									
5									
6									
7									
8									
9									
10									
11									
12									
13									
14									
15									

DISPOSITION

	SELL PRICE (optional)	DATE	NAME	NICS NUMBER (optional)	ADDRESS OR LICENSE NO. OF LICENSEE, OR FORM 4473 SERIAL NO. IF FORMS 4473 FILED NUMERICALLY
1					
2					
3					
4					
5					
6					
7					
8					
9					
10					
11					
12					
13					
14					
15					

ACQUISITION

	DESCRIPTION OF FIREARM					RECEIPT			
	MANUFACTURER AND/ OR IMPORTER	MODEL	SERIAL NO.	TYPE	CALIBER OR GAUGE	DATE	TAG (optional)	COST (optional)	NAME AND ADDRESS OR NAME AND LICENSE NO.
16									
17									
18									
19									
20									
21									
22									
23									
24									
25									
26									
27									
28									
29									
30									

DISPOSITION

	SELL PRICE (optional)	DATE	NAME	NICS NUMBER (optional)	ADDRESS OR LICENSE NO. OF LICENSEE, OR FORM 4473 SERIAL NO. IF FORMS 4473 FILED NUMERICALLY
16					
17					
18					
19					
20					
21					
22					
23					
24					
25					
26					
27					
28					
29					
30					

ACQUISITION

	DESCRIPTION OF FIREARM					RECEIPT			
	MANUFACTURER AND/ OR IMPORTER	MODEL	SERIAL NO.	TYPE	CALIBER OR GAUGE	DATE	TAG (optional)	COST (optional)	NAME AND ADDRESS OR NAME AND LICENSE NO.
31									
32									
33									
34									
35									
36									
37									
38									
39									
40									
41									
42									
43									
44									
45									

DISPOSITION

	SELL PRICE (optional)	DATE	NAME	NICS NUMBER (optional)	ADDRESS OR LICENSE NO. OF LICENSEE, OR FORM 4473 SERIAL NO. IF FORMS 4473 FILED NUMERICALLY
31					
32					
33					
34					
35					
36					
37					
38					
39					
40					
41					
42					
43					
44					
45					

ACQUISITION

	DESCRIPTION OF FIREARM					RECEIPT			
	MANUFACTURER AND/ OR IMPORTER	MODEL	SERIAL NO.	TYPE	CALIBER OR GAUGE	DATE	TAG (optional)	COST (optional)	NAME AND ADDRESS OR NAME AND LICENSE NO.
46									
47									
48									
49									
50									
51									
52									
53									
54									
55									
56									
57									
58									
59									
60									

DISPOSITION

	SELL PRICE (optional)	DATE	NAME	NICS NUMBER (optional)	ADDRESS OR LICENSE NO. OF LICENSEE, OR FORM 4473 SERIAL NO. IF FORMS 4473 FILED NUMERICALLY
46					
47					
48					
49					
50					
51					
52					
53					
54					
55					
56					
57					
58					
59					
60					

ACQUISITION

	DESCRIPTION OF FIREARM					RECEIPT			
	MANUFACTURER AND/ OR IMPORTER	MODEL	SERIAL NO.	TYPE	CALIBER OR GAUGE	DATE	TAG (optional)	COST (optional)	NAME AND ADDRESS OR NAME AND LICENSE NO.
61									
62									
63									
64									
65									
66									
67									
68									
69									
70									
71									
72									
73									
74									
75									

DISPOSITION

	SELL PRICE (optional)	DATE	NAME	NICS NUMBER (optional)	ADDRESS OR LICENSE NO. OF LICENSEE, OR FORM 4473 SERIAL NO. IF FORMS 4473 FILED NUMERICALLY
61					
62					
63					
64					
65					
66					
67					
68					
69					
70					
71					
72					
73					
74					
75					

ACQUISITION

	DESCRIPTION OF FIREARM					RECEIPT			
	MANUFACTURER AND/ OR IMPORTER	MODEL	SERIAL NO.	TYPE	CALIBER OR GAUGE	DATE	TAG (optional)	COST (optional)	NAME AND ADDRESS OR NAME AND LICENSE NO.
76									
77									
78									
79									
80									
81									
82									
83									
84									
85									
86									
87									
88									
89									
90									

DISPOSITION

	SELL PRICE (optional)	DATE	NAME	NICS NUMBER (optional)	ADDRESS OR LICENSE NO. OF LICENSEE, OR FORM 4473 SERIAL NO. IF FORMS 4473 FILED NUMERICALLY
76					
77					
78					
79					
80					
81					
82					
83					
84					
85					
86					
87					
88					
89					
90					

ACQUISITION

	DESCRIPTION OF FIREARM					RECEIPT			
	MANUFACTURER AND/ OR IMPORTER	MODEL	SERIAL NO.	TYPE	CALIBER OR GAUGE	DATE	TAG (optional)	COST (optional)	NAME AND ADDRESS OR NAME AND LICENSE NO.
91									
92									
93									
94									
95									
96									
97									
98									
99									
100									
101									
102									
103									
104									
105									

DISPOSITION

	SELL PRICE (optional)	DATE	NAME	NICS NUMBER (optional)	ADDRESS OR LICENSE NO. OF LICENSEE, OR FORM 4473 SERIAL NO. IF FORMS 4473 FILED NUMERICALLY
91					
92					
93					
94					
95					
96					
97					
98					
99					
100					
101					
102					
103					
104					
105					

ACQUISITION

	DESCRIPTION OF FIREARM					RECEIPT			
	MANUFACTURER AND/ OR IMPORTER	MODEL	SERIAL NO.	TYPE	CALIBER OR GAUGE	DATE	TAG (optional)	COST (optional)	NAME AND ADDRESS OR NAME AND LICENSE NO.
106									
107									
108									
109									
110									
111									
112									
113									
114									
115									
116									
117									
118									
119									
120									

DISPOSITION

	SELL PRICE (optional)	DATE	NAME	NICS NUMBER (optional)	ADDRESS OR LICENSE NO. OF LICENSEE, OR FORM 4473 SERIAL NO. IF FORMS 4473 FILED NUMERICALLY
106					
107					
108					
109					
110					
111					
112					
113					
114					
115					
116					
117					
118					
119					
120					

ACQUISITION

	DESCRIPTION OF FIREARM					RECEIPT			
	MANUFACTURER AND/ OR IMPORTER	MODEL	SERIAL NO.	TYPE	CALIBER OR GAUGE	DATE	TAG (optional)	COST (optional)	NAME AND ADDRESS OR NAME AND LICENSE NO.
121									
122									
123									
124									
125									
126									
127									
128									
129									
130									
131									
132									
133									
134									
135									

DISPOSITION

	SELL PRICE (optional)	DATE	NAME	NICS NUMBER (optional)	ADDRESS OR LICENSE NO. OF LICENSEE, OR FORM 4473 SERIAL NO. IF FORMS 4473 FILED NUMERICALLY
121					
122					
123					
124					
125					
126					
127					
128					
129					
130					
131					
132					
133					
134					
135					

ACQUISITION

	DESCRIPTION OF FIREARM					RECEIPT			
	MANUFACTURER AND/ OR IMPORTER	MODEL	SERIAL NO.	TYPE	CALIBER OR GAUGE	DATE	TAG (optional)	COST (optional)	NAME AND ADDRESS OR NAME AND LICENSE NO.
136									
137									
138									
139									
140									
141									
142									
143									
144									
145									
146									
147									
148									
149									
150									

DISPOSITION

	SELL PRICE (optional)	DATE	NAME	NICS NUMBER (optional)	ADDRESS OR LICENSE NO. OF LICENSEE, OR FORM 4473 SERIAL NO. IF FORMS 4473 FILED NUMERICALLY
136					
137					
138					
139					
140					
141					
142					
143					
144					
145					
146					
147					
148					
149					
150					

ACQUISITION

	DESCRIPTION OF FIREARM					RECEIPT			
	MANUFACTURER AND/ OR IMPORTER	MODEL	SERIAL NO.	TYPE	CALIBER OR GAUGE	DATE	TAG (optional)	COST (optional)	NAME AND ADDRESS OR NAME AND LICENSE NO.
151									
152									
153									
154									
155									
156									
157									
158									
159									
160									
161									
162									
163									
164									
165									

DISPOSITION

	SELL PRICE (optional)	DATE	NAME	NICS NUMBER (optional)	ADDRESS OR LICENSE NO. OF LICENSEE, OR FORM 4473 SERIAL NO. IF FORMS 4473 FILED NUMERICALLY
151					
152					
153					
154					
155					
156					
157					
158					
159					
160					
161					
162					
163					
164					
165					

ACQUISITION

	DESCRIPTION OF FIREARM					RECEIPT			
	MANUFACTURER AND/ OR IMPORTER	MODEL	SERIAL NO.	TYPE	CALIBER OR GAUGE	DATE	TAG (optional)	COST (optional)	NAME AND ADDRESS OR NAME AND LICENSE NO.
166									
167									
168									
169									
170									
171									
172									
173									
174									
175									
176									
177									
178									
179									
180									

DISPOSITION

	SELL PRICE (optional)	DATE	NAME	NICS NUMBER (optional)	ADDRESS OR LICENSE NO. OF LICENSEE, OR FORM 4473 SERIAL NO. IF FORMS 4473 FILED NUMERICALLY
166					
167					
168					
169					
170					
171					
172					
173					
174					
175					
176					
177					
178					
179					
180					

ACQUISITION

	DESCRIPTION OF FIREARM					RECEIPT			
	MANUFACTURER AND/ OR IMPORTER	MODEL	SERIAL NO.	TYPE	CALIBER OR GAUGE	DATE	TAG (optional)	COST (optional)	NAME AND ADDRESS OR NAME AND LICENSE NO.
181									
182									
183									
184									
185									
186									
187									
188									
189									
190									
191									
192									
193									
194									
195									

DISPOSITION

	SELL PRICE (optional)	DATE	NAME	NICS NUMBER (optional)	ADDRESS OR LICENSE NO. OF LICENSEE, OR FORM 4473 SERIAL NO. IF FORMS 4473 FILED NUMERICALLY
181					
182					
183					
184					
185					
186					
187					
188					
189					
190					
191					
192					
193					
194					
195					

ACQUISITION

	DESCRIPTION OF FIREARM					RECEIPT			
	MANUFACTURER AND/ OR IMPORTER	MODEL	SERIAL NO.	TYPE	CALIBER OR GAUGE	DATE	TAG (optional)	COST (optional)	NAME AND ADDRESS OR NAME AND LICENSE NO.
196									
197									
198									
199									
200									
201									
202									
203									
204									
205									
206									
207									
208									
209									
210									

DISPOSITION

	SELL PRICE (optional)	DATE	NAME	NICS NUMBER (optional)	ADDRESS OR LICENSE NO. OF LICENSEE, OR FORM 4473 SERIAL NO. IF FORMS 4473 FILED NUMERICALLY
196					
197					
198					
199					
200					
201					
202					
203					
204					
205					
206					
207					
208					
209					
210					

ACQUISITION

	DESCRIPTION OF FIREARM					RECEIPT			
	MANUFACTURER AND/ OR IMPORTER	MODEL	SERIAL NO.	TYPE	CALIBER OR GAUGE	DATE	TAG (optional)	COST (optional)	NAME AND ADDRESS OR NAME AND LICENSE NO.
211									
212									
213									
214									
215									
216									
217									
218									
219									
220									
221									
222									
223									
224									
225									

DISPOSITION

	SELL PRICE (optional)	DATE	NAME	NICS NUMBER (optional)	ADDRESS OR LICENSE NO. OF LICENSEE, OR FORM 4473 SERIAL NO. IF FORMS 4473 FILED NUMERICALLY
211					
212					
213					
214					
215					
216					
217					
218					
219					
220					
221					
222					
223					
224					
225					

ACQUISITION

	DESCRIPTION OF FIREARM					RECEIPT			
	MANUFACTURER AND/ OR IMPORTER	MODEL	SERIAL NO.	TYPE	CALIBER OR GAUGE	DATE	TAG (optional)	COST (optional)	NAME AND ADDRESS OR NAME AND LICENSE NO.
226									
227									
228									
229									
230									
231									
232									
233									
234									
235									
236									
237									
238									
239									
240									

DISPOSITION

	SELL PRICE (optional)	DATE	NAME	NICS NUMBER (optional)	ADDRESS OR LICENSE NO. OF LICENSEE, OR FORM 4473 SERIAL NO. IF FORMS 4473 FILED NUMERICALLY
226					
227					
228					
229					
230					
231					
232					
233					
234					
235					
236					
237					
238					
239					
240					

ACQUISITION

	DESCRIPTION OF FIREARM					RECEIPT			
	MANUFACTURER AND/ OR IMPORTER	MODEL	SERIAL NO.	TYPE	CALIBER OR GAUGE	DATE	TAG (optional)	COST (optional)	NAME AND ADDRESS OR NAME AND LICENSE NO.
241									
242									
243									
244									
245									
246									
247									
248									
249									
250									
251									
252									
253									
254									
255									

DISPOSITION

	SELL PRICE (optional)	DATE	NAME	NICS NUMBER (optional)	ADDRESS OR LICENSE NO. OF LICENSEE, OR FORM 4473 SERIAL NO. IF FORMS 4473 FILED NUMERICALLY
241					
242					
243					
244					
245					
246					
247					
248					
249					
250					
251					
252					
253					
254					
255					

ACQUISITION

	DESCRIPTION OF FIREARM					RECEIPT			
	MANUFACTURER AND/ OR IMPORTER	MODEL	SERIAL NO.	TYPE	CALIBER OR GAUGE	DATE	TAG (optional)	COST (optional)	NAME AND ADDRESS OR NAME AND LICENSE NO.
256									
257									
258									
259									
260									
261									
262									
263									
264									
265									
266									
267									
268									
269									
270									

DISPOSITION

	SELL PRICE (optional)	DATE	NAME	NICS NUMBER (optional)	ADDRESS OR LICENSE NO. OF LICENSEE, OR FORM 4473 SERIAL NO. IF FORMS 4473 FILED NUMERICALLY
256					
257					
258					
259					
260					
261					
262					
263					
264					
265					
266					
267					
268					
269					
270					

ACQUISITION

	DESCRIPTION OF FIREARM					RECEIPT			
	MANUFACTURER AND/ OR IMPORTER	MODEL	SERIAL NO.	TYPE	CALIBER OR GAUGE	DATE	TAG (optional)	COST (optional)	NAME AND ADDRESS OR NAME AND LICENSE NO.
271									
272									
273									
274									
275									
276									
277									
278									
279									
280									
281									
282									
283									
284									
285									

DISPOSITION

	SELL PRICE (optional)	DATE	NAME	NICS NUMBER (optional)	ADDRESS OR LICENSE NO. OF LICENSEE, OR FORM 4473 SERIAL NO. IF FORMS 4473 FILED NUMERICALLY
271					
272					
273					
274					
275					
276					
277					
278					
279					
280					
281					
282					
283					
284					
285					

ACQUISITION

	DESCRIPTION OF FIREARM					RECEIPT			
	MANUFACTURER AND/ OR IMPORTER	MODEL	SERIAL NO.	TYPE	CALIBER OR GAUGE	DATE	TAG (optional)	COST (optional)	NAME AND ADDRESS OR NAME AND LICENSE NO.
286									
287									
288									
289									
290									
291									
292									
293									
294									
295									
296									
297									
298									
299									
300									

DISPOSITION

	SELL PRICE (optional)	DATE	NAME	NICS NUMBER (optional)	ADDRESS OR LICENSE NO. OF LICENSEE, OR FORM 4473 SERIAL NO. IF FORMS 4473 FILED NUMERICALLY
286					
287					
288					
289					
290					
291					
292					
293					
294					
295					
296					
297					
298					
299					
300					

ACQUISITION

	DESCRIPTION OF FIREARM					RECEIPT			
	MANUFACTURER AND/ OR IMPORTER	MODEL	SERIAL NO.	TYPE	CALIBER OR GAUGE	DATE	TAG (optional)	COST (optional)	NAME AND ADDRESS OR NAME AND LICENSE NO.
301									
302									
303									
304									
305									
306									
307									
308									
309									
310									
311									
312									
313									
314									
315									

DISPOSITION

	SELL PRICE (optional)	DATE	NAME	NICS NUMBER (optional)	ADDRESS OR LICENSE NO. OF LICENSEE, OR FORM 4473 SERIAL NO. IF FORMS 4473 FILED NUMERICALLY
301					
302					
303					
304					
305					
306					
307					
308					
309					
310					
311					
312					
313					
314					
315					

ACQUISITION

	DESCRIPTION OF FIREARM					RECEIPT			
	MANUFACTURER AND/ OR IMPORTER	MODEL	SERIAL NO.	TYPE	CALIBER OR GAUGE	DATE	TAG (optional)	COST (optional)	NAME AND ADDRESS OR NAME AND LICENSE NO.
316									
317									
318									
319									
320									
321									
322									
323									
324									
325									
326									
327									
328									
329									
330									

DISPOSITION

	SELL PRICE (optional)	DATE	NAME	NICS NUMBER (optional)	ADDRESS OR LICENSE NO. OF LICENSEE, OR FORM 4473 SERIAL NO. IF FORMS 4473 FILED NUMERICALLY
316					
317					
318					
319					
320					
321					
322					
323					
324					
325					
326					
327					
328					
329					
330					

ACQUISITION

	DESCRIPTION OF FIREARM					RECEIPT			
	MANUFACTURER AND/ OR IMPORTER	MODEL	SERIAL NO.	TYPE	CALIBER OR GAUGE	DATE	TAG (optional)	COST (optional)	NAME AND ADDRESS OR NAME AND LICENSE NO.
331									
332									
333									
334									
335									
336									
337									
338									
339									
340									
341									
342									
343									
344									
345									

DISPOSITION

	SELL PRICE (optional)	DATE	NAME	NICS NUMBER (optional)	ADDRESS OR LICENSE NO. OF LICENSEE, OR FORM 4473 SERIAL NO. IF FORMS 4473 FILED NUMERICALLY
331					
332					
333					
334					
335					
336					
337					
338					
339					
340					
341					
342					
343					
344					
345					

ACQUISITION

	DESCRIPTION OF FIREARM					RECEIPT			
	MANUFACTURER AND/ OR IMPORTER	MODEL	SERIAL NO.	TYPE	CALIBER OR GAUGE	DATE	TAG (optional)	COST (optional)	NAME AND ADDRESS OR NAME AND LICENSE NO.
346									
347									
348									
349									
350									
351									
352									
353									
354									
355									
356									
357									
358									
359									
360									

DISPOSITION

	SELL PRICE (optional)	DATE	NAME	NICS NUMBER (optional)	ADDRESS OR LICENSE NO. OF LICENSEE, OR FORM 4473 SERIAL NO. IF FORMS 4473 FILED NUMERICALLY
346					
347					
348					
349					
350					
351					
352					
353					
354					
355					
356					
357					
358					
359					
360					

ACQUISITION

	DESCRIPTION OF FIREARM					RECEIPT			
	MANUFACTURER AND/ OR IMPORTER	MODEL	SERIAL NO.	TYPE	CALIBER OR GAUGE	DATE	TAG (optional)	COST (optional)	NAME AND ADDRESS OR NAME AND LICENSE NO.
361									
362									
363									
364									
365									
366									
367									
368									
369									
370									
371									
372									
373									
374									
375									

DISPOSITION

	SELL PRICE (optional)	DATE	NAME	NICS NUMBER (optional)	ADDRESS OR LICENSE NO. OF LICENSEE, OR FORM 4473 SERIAL NO. IF FORMS 4473 FILED NUMERICALLY
361					
362					
363					
364					
365					
366					
367					
368					
369					
370					
371					
372					
373					
374					
375					

ACQUISITION

	DESCRIPTION OF FIREARM					RECEIPT			
	MANUFACTURER AND/ OR IMPORTER	MODEL	SERIAL NO.	TYPE	CALIBER OR GAUGE	DATE	TAG (optional)	COST (optional)	NAME AND ADDRESS OR NAME AND LICENSE NO.
376									
377									
378									
379									
380									
381									
382									
383									
384									
385									
386									
387									
388									
389									
390									

DISPOSITION

	SELL PRICE (optional)	DATE	NAME	NICS NUMBER (optional)	ADDRESS OR LICENSE NO. OF LICENSEE, OR FORM 4473 SERIAL NO. IF FORMS 4473 FILED NUMERICALLY
376					
377					
378					
379					
380					
381					
382					
383					
384					
385					
386					
387					
388					
389					
390					

ACQUISITION

	DESCRIPTION OF FIREARM					RECEIPT			
	MANUFACTURER AND/ OR IMPORTER	MODEL	SERIAL NO.	TYPE	CALIBER OR GAUGE	DATE	TAG (optional)	COST (optional)	NAME AND ADDRESS OR NAME AND LICENSE NO.
391									
392									
393									
394									
395									
396									
397									
398									
399									
400									
401									
402									
403									
404									
405									

DISPOSITION

	SELL PRICE (optional)	DATE	NAME	NICS NUMBER (optional)	ADDRESS OR LICENSE NO. OF LICENSEE, OR FORM 4473 SERIAL NO. IF FORMS 4473 FILED NUMERICALLY
391					
392					
393					
394					
395					
396					
397					
398					
399					
400					
401					
402					
403					
404					
405					

ACQUISITION

	DESCRIPTION OF FIREARM					RECEIPT			
	MANUFACTURER AND/ OR IMPORTER	MODEL	SERIAL NO.	TYPE	CALIBER OR GAUGE	DATE	TAG (optional)	COST (optional)	NAME AND ADDRESS OR NAME AND LICENSE NO.
406									
407									
408									
409									
410									
411									
412									
413									
414									
415									
416									
417									
418									
419									
420									

DISPOSITION

	SELL PRICE (optional)	DATE	NAME	NICS NUMBER (optional)	ADDRESS OR LICENSE NO. OF LICENSEE, OR FORM 4473 SERIAL NO. IF FORMS 4473 FILED NUMERICALLY
406					
407					
408					
409					
410					
411					
412					
413					
414					
415					
416					
417					
418					
419					
420					

ACQUISITION

	DESCRIPTION OF FIREARM					RECEIPT			
	MANUFACTURER AND/ OR IMPORTER	MODEL	SERIAL NO.	TYPE	CALIBER OR GAUGE	DATE	TAG (optional)	COST (optional)	NAME AND ADDRESS OR NAME AND LICENSE NO.
421									
422									
423									
424									
425									
426									
427									
428									
429									
430									
431									
432									
433									
434									
435									

DISPOSITION

	SELL PRICE (optional)	DATE	NAME	NICS NUMBER (optional)	ADDRESS OR LICENSE NO. OF LICENSEE, OR FORM 4473 SERIAL NO. IF FORMS 4473 FILED NUMERICALLY
421					
422					
423					
424					
425					
426					
427					
428					
429					
430					
431					
432					
433					
434					
435					

ACQUISITION

	DESCRIPTION OF FIREARM					RECEIPT			
	MANUFACTURER AND/ OR IMPORTER	MODEL	SERIAL NO.	TYPE	CALIBER OR GAUGE	DATE	TAG (optional)	COST (optional)	NAME AND ADDRESS OR NAME AND LICENSE NO.
436									
437									
438									
439									
440									
441									
442									
443									
444									
445									
446									
447									
448									
449									
450									

DISPOSITION

	SELL PRICE (optional)	DATE	NAME	NICS NUMBER (optional)	ADDRESS OR LICENSE NO. OF LICENSEE, OR FORM 4473 SERIAL NO. IF FORMS 4473 FILED NUMERICALLY
436					
437					
438					
439					
440					
441					
442					
443					
444					
445					
446					
447					
448					
449					
450					

ACQUISITION

	DESCRIPTION OF FIREARM					RECEIPT			
	MANUFACTURER AND/ OR IMPORTER	MODEL	SERIAL NO.	TYPE	CALIBER OR GAUGE	DATE	TAG (optional)	COST (optional)	NAME AND ADDRESS OR NAME AND LICENSE NO.
451									
452									
453									
454									
455									
456									
457									
458									
459									
460									
461									
462									
463									
464									
465									

DISPOSITION

	SELL PRICE (optional)	DATE	NAME	NICS NUMBER (optional)	ADDRESS OR LICENSE NO. OF LICENSEE, OR FORM 4473 SERIAL NO. IF FORMS 4473 FILED NUMERICALLY
451					
452					
453					
454					
455					
456					
457					
458					
459					
460					
461					
462					
463					
464					
465					

ACQUISITION

	DESCRIPTION OF FIREARM					RECEIPT			
	MANUFACTURER AND/ OR IMPORTER	MODEL	SERIAL NO.	TYPE	CALIBER OR GAUGE	DATE	TAG (optional)	COST (optional)	NAME AND ADDRESS OR NAME AND LICENSE NO.
466									
467									
468									
469									
470									
471									
472									
473									
474									
475									
476									
477									
478									
479									
480									

DISPOSITION

	SELL PRICE (optional)	DATE	NAME	NICS NUMBER (optional)	ADDRESS OR LICENSE NO. OF LICENSEE, OR FORM 4473 SERIAL NO. IF FORMS 4473 FILED NUMERICALLY
466					
467					
468					
469					
470					
471					
472					
473					
474					
475					
476					
477					
478					
479					
480					

ACQUISITION

	DESCRIPTION OF FIREARM					RECEIPT			
	MANUFACTURER AND/ OR IMPORTER	MODEL	SERIAL NO.	TYPE	CALIBER OR GAUGE	DATE	TAG (optional)	COST (optional)	NAME AND ADDRESS OR NAME AND LICENSE NO.
481									
482									
483									
484									
485									
486									
487									
488									
489									
490									
491									
492									
493									
494									
495									

DISPOSITION

	SELL PRICE (optional)	DATE	NAME	NICS NUMBER (optional)	ADDRESS OR LICENSE NO. OF LICENSEE, OR FORM 4473 SERIAL NO. IF FORMS 4473 FILED NUMERICALLY
481					
482					
483					
484					
485					
486					
487					
488					
489					
490					
491					
492					
493					
494					
495					

ACQUISITION

	DESCRIPTION OF FIREARM					RECEIPT			
	MANUFACTURER AND/ OR IMPORTER	MODEL	SERIAL NO.	TYPE	CALIBER OR GAUGE	DATE	TAG (optional)	COST (optional)	NAME AND ADDRESS OR NAME AND LICENSE NO.
496									
497									
498									
499									
500									
501									
502									
503									
504									
505									
506									
507									
508									
509									
510									

DISPOSITION

	SELL PRICE (optional)	DATE	NAME	NICS NUMBER (optional)	ADDRESS OR LICENSE NO. OF LICENSEE, OR FORM 4473 SERIAL NO. IF FORMS 4473 FILED NUMERICALLY
496					
497					
498					
499					
500					
501					
502					
503					
504					
505					
506					
507					
508					
509					
510					

ACQUISITION

	DESCRIPTION OF FIREARM					RECEIPT			
	MANUFACTURER AND/ OR IMPORTER	MODEL	SERIAL NO.	TYPE	CALIBER OR GAUGE	DATE	TAG (optional)	COST (optional)	NAME AND ADDRESS OR NAME AND LICENSE NO.
511									
512									
513									
514									
515									
516									
517									
518									
519									
520									
521									
522									
523									
524									
525									

DISPOSITION

	SELL PRICE (optional)	DATE	NAME	NICS NUMBER (optional)	ADDRESS OR LICENSE NO. OF LICENSEE, OR FORM 4473 SERIAL NO. IF FORMS 4473 FILED NUMERICALLY
511					
512					
513					
514					
515					
516					
517					
518					
519					
520					
521					
522					
523					
524					
525					

ACQUISITION

	DESCRIPTION OF FIREARM					RECEIPT			
	MANUFACTURER AND/ OR IMPORTER	MODEL	SERIAL NO.	TYPE	CALIBER OR GAUGE	DATE	TAG (optional)	COST (optional)	NAME AND ADDRESS OR NAME AND LICENSE NO.
526									
527									
528									
529									
530									
531									
532									
533									
534									
535									
536									
537									
538									
539									
540									

DISPOSITION

	SELL PRICE (optional)	DATE	NAME	NICS NUMBER (optional)	ADDRESS OR LICENSE NO. OF LICENSEE, OR FORM 4473 SERIAL NO. IF FORMS 4473 FILED NUMERICALLY
526					
527					
528					
529					
530					
531					
532					
533					
534					
535					
536					
537					
538					
539					
540					

ACQUISITION

	DESCRIPTION OF FIREARM					RECEIPT			
	MANUFACTURER AND/ OR IMPORTER	MODEL	SERIAL NO.	TYPE	CALIBER OR GAUGE	DATE	TAG (optional)	COST (optional)	NAME AND ADDRESS OR NAME AND LICENSE NO.
541									
542									
543									
544									
545									
546									
547									
548									
549									
550									
551									
552									
553									
554									
555									

DISPOSITION

	SELL PRICE (optional)	DATE	NAME	NICS NUMBER (optional)	ADDRESS OR LICENSE NO. OF LICENSEE, OR FORM 4473 SERIAL NO. IF FORMS 4473 FILED NUMERICALLY
541					
542					
543					
544					
545					
546					
547					
548					
549					
550					
551					
552					
553					
554					
555					

ACQUISITION

	DESCRIPTION OF FIREARM					RECEIPT			
	MANUFACTURER AND/ OR IMPORTER	MODEL	SERIAL NO.	TYPE	CALIBER OR GAUGE	DATE	TAG (optional)	COST (optional)	NAME AND ADDRESS OR NAME AND LICENSE NO.
556									
557									
558									
559									
560									
561									
562									
563									
564									
565									
566									
567									
568									
569									
570									

DISPOSITION

	SELL PRICE (optional)	DATE	NAME	NICS NUMBER (optional)	ADDRESS OR LICENSE NO. OF LICENSEE, OR FORM 4473 SERIAL NO. IF FORMS 4473 FILED NUMERICALLY
556					
557					
558					
559					
560					
561					
562					
563					
564					
565					
566					
567					
568					
569					
570					

ACQUISITION

	DESCRIPTION OF FIREARM					RECEIPT			
	MANUFACTURER AND/ OR IMPORTER	MODEL	SERIAL NO.	TYPE	CALIBER OR GAUGE	DATE	TAG (optional)	COST (optional)	NAME AND ADDRESS OR NAME AND LICENSE NO.
571									
572									
573									
574									
575									
576									
577									
578									
579									
580									
581									
582									
583									
584									
585									

DISPOSITION

	SELL PRICE (optional)	DATE	NAME	NICS NUMBER (optional)	ADDRESS OR LICENSE NO. OF LICENSEE, OR FORM 4473 SERIAL NO. IF FORMS 4473 FILED NUMERICALLY
571					
572					
573					
574					
575					
576					
577					
578					
579					
580					
581					
582					
583					
584					
585					

ACQUISITION

	DESCRIPTION OF FIREARM					RECEIPT			
	MANUFACTURER AND/ OR IMPORTER	MODEL	SERIAL NO.	TYPE	CALIBER OR GAUGE	DATE	TAG (optional)	COST (optional)	NAME AND ADDRESS OR NAME AND LICENSE NO.
586									
587									
588									
589									
590									
591									
592									
593									
594									
595									
596									
597									
598									
599									
600									

DISPOSITION

	SELL PRICE (optional)	DATE	NAME	NICS NUMBER (optional)	ADDRESS OR LICENSE NO. OF LICENSEE, OR FORM 4473 SERIAL NO. IF FORMS 4473 FILED NUMERICALLY
586					
587					
588					
589					
590					
591					
592					
593					
594					
595					
596					
597					
598					
599					
600					

ACQUISITION

	DESCRIPTION OF FIREARM					RECEIPT			
	MANUFACTURER AND/ OR IMPORTER	MODEL	SERIAL NO.	TYPE	CALIBER OR GAUGE	DATE	TAG (optional)	COST (optional)	NAME AND ADDRESS OR NAME AND LICENSE NO.
601									
602									
603									
604									
605									
606									
607									
608									
609									
610									
611									
612									
613									
614									
615									

DISPOSITION

	SELL PRICE (optional)	DATE	NAME	NICS NUMBER (optional)	ADDRESS OR LICENSE NO. OF LICENSEE, OR FORM 4473 SERIAL NO. IF FORMS 4473 FILED NUMERICALLY
601					
602					
603					
604					
605					
606					
607					
608					
609					
610					
611					
612					
613					
614					
615					

ACQUISITION

	DESCRIPTION OF FIREARM					RECEIPT			
	MANUFACTURER AND/ OR IMPORTER	MODEL	SERIAL NO.	TYPE	CALIBER OR GAUGE	DATE	TAG (optional)	COST (optional)	NAME AND ADDRESS OR NAME AND LICENSE NO.
616									
617									
618									
619									
620									
621									
622									
623									
624									
625									
626									
627									
628									
629									
630									

DISPOSITION

	SELL PRICE (optional)	DATE	NAME	NICS NUMBER (optional)	ADDRESS OR LICENSE NO. OF LICENSEE, OR FORM 4473 SERIAL NO. IF FORMS 4473 FILED NUMERICALLY
616					
617					
618					
619					
620					
621					
622					
623					
624					
625					
626					
627					
628					
629					
630					

ACQUISITION

	DESCRIPTION OF FIREARM					RECEIPT			
	MANUFACTURER AND/ OR IMPORTER	MODEL	SERIAL NO.	TYPE	CALIBER OR GAUGE	DATE	TAG (optional)	COST (optional)	NAME AND ADDRESS OR NAME AND LICENSE NO.
631									
632									
633									
634									
635									
636									
637									
638									
639									
640									
641									
642									
643									
644									
645									

DISPOSITION

	SELL PRICE (optional)	DATE	NAME	NICS NUMBER (optional)	ADDRESS OR LICENSE NO. OF LICENSEE, OR FORM 4473 SERIAL NO. IF FORMS 4473 FILED NUMERICALLY
631					
632					
633					
634					
635					
636					
637					
638					
639					
640					
641					
642					
643					
644					
645					

ACQUISITION

	DESCRIPTION OF FIREARM					RECEIPT			
	MANUFACTURER AND/ OR IMPORTER	MODEL	SERIAL NO.	TYPE	CALIBER OR GAUGE	DATE	TAG (optional)	COST (optional)	NAME AND ADDRESS OR NAME AND LICENSE NO.
646									
647									
648									
649									
650									
651									
652									
653									
654									
655									
656									
657									
658									
659									
660									

DISPOSITION

	SELL PRICE (optional)	DATE	NAME	NICS NUMBER (optional)	ADDRESS OR LICENSE NO. OF LICENSEE, OR FORM 4473 SERIAL NO. IF FORMS 4473 FILED NUMERICALLY
646					
647					
648					
649					
650					
651					
652					
653					
654					
655					
656					
657					
658					
659					
660					

ACQUISITION

	DESCRIPTION OF FIREARM					RECEIPT			
	MANUFACTURER AND/ OR IMPORTER	MODEL	SERIAL NO.	TYPE	CALIBER OR GAUGE	DATE	TAG (optional)	COST (optional)	NAME AND ADDRESS OR NAME AND LICENSE NO.
661									
662									
663									
664									
665									
666									
667									
668									
669									
670									
671									
672									
673									
674									
675									

DISPOSITION

	SELL PRICE (optional)	DATE	NAME	NICS NUMBER (optional)	ADDRESS OR LICENSE NO. OF LICENSEE, OR FORM 4473 SERIAL NO. IF FORMS 4473 FILED NUMERICALLY
661					
662					
663					
664					
665					
666					
667					
668					
669					
670					
671					
672					
673					
674					
675					

ACQUISITION

	DESCRIPTION OF FIREARM					RECEIPT			
	MANUFACTURER AND/ OR IMPORTER	MODEL	SERIAL NO.	TYPE	CALIBER OR GAUGE	DATE	TAG (optional)	COST (optional)	NAME AND ADDRESS OR NAME AND LICENSE NO.
676									
677									
678									
679									
680									
681									
682									
683									
684									
685									
686									
687									
688									
689									
690									

DISPOSITION

	SELL PRICE (optional)	DATE	NAME	NICS NUMBER (optional)	ADDRESS OR LICENSE NO. OF LICENSEE, OR FORM 4473 SERIAL NO. IF FORMS 4473 FILED NUMERICALLY
676					
677					
678					
679					
680					
681					
682					
683					
684					
685					
686					
687					
688					
689					
690					

ACQUISITION

	DESCRIPTION OF FIREARM					RECEIPT			
	MANUFACTURER AND/ OR IMPORTER	MODEL	SERIAL NO.	TYPE	CALIBER OR GAUGE	DATE	TAG (optional)	COST (optional)	NAME AND ADDRESS OR NAME AND LICENSE NO.
691									
692									
693									
694									
695									
696									
697									
698									
699									
700									
701									
702									
703									
704									
705									

DISPOSITION

	SELL PRICE (optional)	DATE	NAME	NICS NUMBER (optional)	ADDRESS OR LICENSE NO. OF LICENSEE, OR FORM 4473 SERIAL NO. IF FORMS 4473 FILED NUMERICALLY
691					
692					
693					
694					
695					
696					
697					
698					
699					
700					
701					
702					
703					
704					
705					

ACQUISITION

	DESCRIPTION OF FIREARM					RECEIPT			
	MANUFACTURER AND/ OR IMPORTER	MODEL	SERIAL NO.	TYPE	CALIBER OR GAUGE	DATE	TAG (optional)	COST (optional)	NAME AND ADDRESS OR NAME AND LICENSE NO.
706									
707									
708									
709									
710									
711									
712									
713									
714									
715									
716									
717									
718									
719									
720									

DISPOSITION

	SELL PRICE (optional)	DATE	NAME	NICS NUMBER (optional)	ADDRESS OR LICENSE NO. OF LICENSEE, OR FORM 4473 SERIAL NO. IF FORMS 4473 FILED NUMERICALLY
706					
707					
708					
709					
710					
711					
712					
713					
714					
715					
716					
717					
718					
719					
720					

ACQUISITION

	DESCRIPTION OF FIREARM					RECEIPT			
	MANUFACTURER AND/ OR IMPORTER	MODEL	SERIAL NO.	TYPE	CALIBER OR GAUGE	DATE	TAG (optional)	COST (optional)	NAME AND ADDRESS OR NAME AND LICENSE NO.
721									
722									
723									
724									
725									
726									
727									
728									
729									
730									
731									
732									
733									
734									
735									

DISPOSITION

	SELL PRICE (optional)	DATE	NAME	NICS NUMBER (optional)	ADDRESS OR LICENSE NO. OF LICENSEE, OR FORM 4473 SERIAL NO. IF FORMS 4473 FILED NUMERICALLY
721					
722					
723					
724					
725					
726					
727					
728					
729					
730					
731					
732					
733					
734					
735					

ACQUISITION

	DESCRIPTION OF FIREARM					RECEIPT			
	MANUFACTURER AND/ OR IMPORTER	MODEL	SERIAL NO.	TYPE	CALIBER OR GAUGE	DATE	TAG (optional)	COST (optional)	NAME AND ADDRESS OR NAME AND LICENSE NO.
736									
737									
738									
739									
740									
741									
742									
743									
744									
745									
746									
747									
748									
749									
750									

DISPOSITION

	SELL PRICE (optional)	DATE	NAME	NICS NUMBER (optional)	ADDRESS OR LICENSE NO. OF LICENSEE, OR FORM 4473 SERIAL NO. IF FORMS 4473 FILED NUMERICALLY
736					
737					
738					
739					
740					
741					
742					
743					
744					
745					
746					
747					
748					
749					
750					

ACQUISITION

	DESCRIPTION OF FIREARM					RECEIPT			
	MANUFACTURER AND/ OR IMPORTER	MODEL	SERIAL NO.	TYPE	CALIBER OR GAUGE	DATE	TAG (optional)	COST (optional)	NAME AND ADDRESS OR NAME AND LICENSE NO.
751									
752									
753									
754									
755									
756									
757									
758									
759									
760									
761									
762									
763									
764									
765									

DISPOSITION

	SELL PRICE (optional)	DATE	NAME	NICS NUMBER (optional)	ADDRESS OR LICENSE NO. OF LICENSEE, OR FORM 4473 SERIAL NO. IF FORMS 4473 FILED NUMERICALLY
751					
752					
753					
754					
755					
756					
757					
758					
759					
760					
761					
762					
763					
764					
765					

ACQUISITION

	DESCRIPTION OF FIREARM					RECEIPT			
	MANUFACTURER AND/ OR IMPORTER	MODEL	SERIAL NO.	TYPE	CALIBER OR GAUGE	DATE	TAG (optional)	COST (optional)	NAME AND ADDRESS OR NAME AND LICENSE NO.
766									
767									
768									
769									
770									
771									
772									
773									
774									
775									
776									
777									
778									
779									
780									

DISPOSITION

	SELL PRICE (optional)	DATE	NAME	NICS NUMBER (optional)	ADDRESS OR LICENSE NO. OF LICENSEE, OR FORM 4473 SERIAL NO. IF FORMS 4473 FILED NUMERICALLY
766					
767					
768					
769					
770					
771					
772					
773					
774					
775					
776					
777					
778					
779					
780					

ACQUISITION

	DESCRIPTION OF FIREARM					RECEIPT			
	MANUFACTURER AND/ OR IMPORTER	MODEL	SERIAL NO.	TYPE	CALIBER OR GAUGE	DATE	TAG (optional)	COST (optional)	NAME AND ADDRESS OR NAME AND LICENSE NO.
781									
782									
783									
784									
785									
786									
787									
788									
789									
790									
791									
792									
793									
794									
795									

DISPOSITION

	SELL PRICE (optional)	DATE	NAME	NICS NUMBER (optional)	ADDRESS OR LICENSE NO. OF LICENSEE, OR FORM 4473 SERIAL NO. IF FORMS 4473 FILED NUMERICALLY
781					
782					
783					
784					
785					
786					
787					
788					
789					
790					
791					
792					
793					
794					
795					

ACQUISITION

	DESCRIPTION OF FIREARM					RECEIPT			
	MANUFACTURER AND/ OR IMPORTER	MODEL	SERIAL NO.	TYPE	CALIBER OR GAUGE	DATE	TAG (optional)	COST (optional)	NAME AND ADDRESS OR NAME AND LICENSE NO.
796									
797									
798									
799									
800									
801									
802									
803									
804									
805									
806									
807									
808									
809									
810									

DISPOSITION

	SELL PRICE (optional)	DATE	NAME	NICS NUMBER (optional)	ADDRESS OR LICENSE NO. OF LICENSEE, OR FORM 4473 SERIAL NO. IF FORMS 4473 FILED NUMERICALLY
796					
797					
798					
799					
800					
801					
802					
803					
804					
805					
806					
807					
808					
809					
810					

ACQUISITION

	DESCRIPTION OF FIREARM					RECEIPT			
	MANUFACTURER AND/ OR IMPORTER	MODEL	SERIAL NO.	TYPE	CALIBER OR GAUGE	DATE	TAG (optional)	COST (optional)	NAME AND ADDRESS OR NAME AND LICENSE NO.
811									
812									
813									
814									
815									
816									
817									
818									
819									
820									
821									
822									
823									
824									
825									

DISPOSITION

	SELL PRICE (optional)	DATE	NAME	NICS NUMBER (optional)	ADDRESS OR LICENSE NO. OF LICENSEE, OR FORM 4473 SERIAL NO. IF FORMS 4473 FILED NUMERICALLY
811					
812					
813					
814					
815					
816					
817					
818					
819					
820					
821					
822					
823					
824					
825					

ACQUISITION

	DESCRIPTION OF FIREARM					RECEIPT			
	MANUFACTURER AND/ OR IMPORTER	MODEL	SERIAL NO.	TYPE	CALIBER OR GAUGE	DATE	TAG (optional)	COST (optional)	NAME AND ADDRESS OR NAME AND LICENSE NO.
826									
827									
828									
829									
830									
831									
832									
833									
834									
835									
836									
837									
838									
839									
840									

DISPOSITION

	SELL PRICE (optional)	DATE	NAME	NICS NUMBER (optional)	ADDRESS OR LICENSE NO. OF LICENSEE, OR FORM 4473 SERIAL NO. IF FORMS 4473 FILED NUMERICALLY
826					
827					
828					
829					
830					
831					
832					
833					
834					
835					
836					
837					
838					
839					
840					

ACQUISITION

	DESCRIPTION OF FIREARM					RECEIPT			
	MANUFACTURER AND/ OR IMPORTER	MODEL	SERIAL NO.	TYPE	CALIBER OR GAUGE	DATE	TAG (optional)	COST (optional)	NAME AND ADDRESS OR NAME AND LICENSE NO.
841									
842									
843									
844									
845									
846									
847									
848									
849									
850									
851									
852									
853									
854									
855									

DISPOSITION

	SELL PRICE (optional)	DATE	NAME	NICS NUMBER (optional)	ADDRESS OR LICENSE NO. OF LICENSEE, OR FORM 4473 SERIAL NO. IF FORMS 4473 FILED NUMERICALLY
841					
842					
843					
844					
845					
846					
847					
848					
849					
850					
851					
852					
853					
854					
855					

ACQUISITION

	DESCRIPTION OF FIREARM					RECEIPT			
	MANUFACTURER AND/ OR IMPORTER	MODEL	SERIAL NO.	TYPE	CALIBER OR GAUGE	DATE	TAG (optional)	COST (optional)	NAME AND ADDRESS OR NAME AND LICENSE NO.
856									
857									
858									
859									
860									
861									
862									
863									
864									
865									
866									
867									
868									
869									
870									

DISPOSITION

	SELL PRICE (optional)	DATE	NAME	NICS NUMBER (optional)	ADDRESS OR LICENSE NO. OF LICENSEE, OR FORM 4473 SERIAL NO. IF FORMS 4473 FILED NUMERICALLY
856					
857					
858					
859					
860					
861					
862					
863					
864					
865					
866					
867					
868					
869					
870					

ACQUISITION

	DESCRIPTION OF FIREARM					RECEIPT			
	MANUFACTURER AND/ OR IMPORTER	MODEL	SERIAL NO.	TYPE	CALIBER OR GAUGE	DATE	TAG (optional)	COST (optional)	NAME AND ADDRESS OR NAME AND LICENSE NO.
871									
872									
873									
874									
875									
876									
877									
878									
879									
880									
881									
882									
883									
884									
885									

DISPOSITION

	SELL PRICE (optional)	DATE	NAME	NICS NUMBER (optional)	ADDRESS OR LICENSE NO. OF LICENSEE, OR FORM 4473 SERIAL NO. IF FORMS 4473 FILED NUMERICALLY
871					
872					
873					
874					
875					
876					
877					
878					
879					
880					
881					
882					
883					
884					
885					

ACQUISITION

	DESCRIPTION OF FIREARM					RECEIPT			
	MANUFACTURER AND/ OR IMPORTER	MODEL	SERIAL NO.	TYPE	CALIBER OR GAUGE	DATE	TAG (optional)	COST (optional)	NAME AND ADDRESS OR NAME AND LICENSE NO.
886									
887									
888									
889									
890									
891									
892									
893									
894									
895									
896									
897									
898									
899									
900									

DISPOSITION

	SELL PRICE (optional)	DATE	NAME	NICS NUMBER (optional)	ADDRESS OR LICENSE NO. OF LICENSEE, OR FORM 4473 SERIAL NO. IF FORMS 4473 FILED NUMERICALLY
886					
887					
888					
889					
890					
891					
892					
893					
894					
895					
896					
897					
898					
899					
900					

ACQUISITION

	DESCRIPTION OF FIREARM					RECEIPT			
	MANUFACTURER AND/ OR IMPORTER	MODEL	SERIAL NO.	TYPE	CALIBER OR GAUGE	DATE	TAG (optional)	COST (optional)	NAME AND ADDRESS OR NAME AND LICENSE NO.
901									
902									
903									
904									
905									
906									
907									
908									
909									
910									
911									
912									
913									
914									
915									

DISPOSITION

	SELL PRICE (optional)	DATE	NAME	NICS NUMBER (optional)	ADDRESS OR LICENSE NO. OF LICENSEE, OR FORM 4473 SERIAL NO. IF FORMS 4473 FILED NUMERICALLY
901					
902					
903					
904					
905					
906					
907					
908					
909					
910					
911					
912					
913					
914					
915					

ACQUISITION

	DESCRIPTION OF FIREARM					RECEIPT			
	MANUFACTURER AND/ OR IMPORTER	MODEL	SERIAL NO.	TYPE	CALIBER OR GAUGE	DATE	TAG (optional)	COST (optional)	NAME AND ADDRESS OR NAME AND LICENSE NO.
916									
917									
918									
919									
920									
921									
922									
923									
924									
925									
926									
927									
928									
929									
930									

DISPOSITION

	SELL PRICE (optional)	DATE	NAME	NICS NUMBER (optional)	ADDRESS OR LICENSE NO. OF LICENSEE, OR FORM 4473 SERIAL NO. IF FORMS 4473 FILED NUMERICALLY
916					
917					
918					
919					
920					
921					
922					
923					
924					
925					
926					
927					
928					
929					
930					

ACQUISITION

	DESCRIPTION OF FIREARM					RECEIPT			
	MANUFACTURER AND/ OR IMPORTER	MODEL	SERIAL NO.	TYPE	CALIBER OR GAUGE	DATE	TAG (optional)	COST (optional)	NAME AND ADDRESS OR NAME AND LICENSE NO.
931									
932									
933									
934									
935									
936									
937									
938									
939									
940									
941									
942									
943									
944									
945									

DISPOSITION

	SELL PRICE (optional)	DATE	NAME	NICS NUMBER (optional)	ADDRESS OR LICENSE NO. OF LICENSEE, OR FORM 4473 SERIAL NO. IF FORMS 4473 FILED NUMERICALLY
931					
932					
933					
934					
935					
936					
937					
938					
939					
940					
941					
942					
943					
944					
945					

ACQUISITION

	DESCRIPTION OF FIREARM					RECEIPT			
	MANUFACTURER AND/ OR IMPORTER	MODEL	SERIAL NO.	TYPE	CALIBER OR GAUGE	DATE	TAG (optional)	COST (optional)	NAME AND ADDRESS OR NAME AND LICENSE NO.
946									
947									
948									
949									
950									
951									
952									
953									
954									
955									
956									
957									
958									
959									
960									

DISPOSITION

	SELL PRICE (optional)	DATE	NAME	NICS NUMBER (optional)	ADDRESS OR LICENSE NO. OF LICENSEE, OR FORM 4473 SERIAL NO. IF FORMS 4473 FILED NUMERICALLY
946					
947					
948					
949					
950					
951					
952					
953					
954					
955					
956					
957					
958					
959					
960					

ACQUISITION

	DESCRIPTION OF FIREARM					RECEIPT			
	MANUFACTURER AND/ OR IMPORTER	MODEL	SERIAL NO.	TYPE	CALIBER OR GAUGE	DATE	TAG (optional)	COST (optional)	NAME AND ADDRESS OR NAME AND LICENSE NO.
961									
962									
963									
964									
965									
966									
967									
968									
969									
970									
971									
972									
973									
974									
975									

DISPOSITION

	SELL PRICE (optional)	DATE	NAME	NICS NUMBER (optional)	ADDRESS OR LICENSE NO. OF LICENSEE, OR FORM 4473 SERIAL NO. IF FORMS 4473 FILED NUMERICALLY
961					
962					
963					
964					
965					
966					
967					
968					
969					
970					
971					
972					
973					
974					
975					

ACQUISITION

	DESCRIPTION OF FIREARM					RECEIPT			
	MANUFACTURER AND/ OR IMPORTER	MODEL	SERIAL NO.	TYPE	CALIBER OR GAUGE	DATE	TAG (optional)	COST (optional)	NAME AND ADDRESS OR NAME AND LICENSE NO.
976									
977									
978									
979									
980									
981									
982									
983									
984									
985									
986									
987									
988									
989									
990									

DISPOSITION

	SELL PRICE (optional)	DATE	NAME	NICS NUMBER (optional)	ADDRESS OR LICENSE NO. OF LICENSEE, OR FORM 4473 SERIAL NO. IF FORMS 4473 FILED NUMERICALLY
976					
977					
978					
979					
980					
981					
982					
983					
984					
985					
986					
987					
988					
989					
990					

ACQUISITION

	DESCRIPTION OF FIREARM					RECEIPT			
	MANUFACTURER AND/ OR IMPORTER	MODEL	SERIAL NO.	TYPE	CALIBER OR GAUGE	DATE	TAG (optional)	COST (optional)	NAME AND ADDRESS OR NAME AND LICENSE NO.
991									
992									
993									
994									
995									
996									
997									
998									
999									
1000									
1001									
1002									
1003									
1004									
1005									

DISPOSITION

	SELL PRICE (optional)	DATE	NAME	NICS NUMBER (optional)	ADDRESS OR LICENSE NO. OF LICENSEE, OR FORM 4473 SERIAL NO. IF FORMS 4473 FILED NUMERICALLY
991					
992					
993					
994					
995					
996					
997					
998					
999					
1000					
1001					
1002					
1003					
1004					
1005					

ACQUISITION

	DESCRIPTION OF FIREARM					RECEIPT			
	MANUFACTURER AND/ OR IMPORTER	MODEL	SERIAL NO.	TYPE	CALIBER OR GAUGE	DATE	TAG (optional)	COST (optional)	NAME AND ADDRESS OR NAME AND LICENSE NO.
1006									
1007									
1008									
1009									
1010									
1011									
1012									
1013									
1014									
1015									
1016									
1017									
1018									
1019									
1020									

DISPOSITION

	SELL PRICE (optional)	DATE	NAME	NICS NUMBER (optional)	ADDRESS OR LICENSE NO. OF LICENSEE, OR FORM 4473 SERIAL NO. IF FORMS 4473 FILED NUMERICALLY
1006					
1007					
1008					
1009					
1010					
1011					
1012					
1013					
1014					
1015					
1016					
1017					
1018					
1019					
1020					

ACQUISITION

	DESCRIPTION OF FIREARM					RECEIPT			
	MANUFACTURER AND/ OR IMPORTER	MODEL	SERIAL NO.	TYPE	CALIBER OR GAUGE	DATE	TAG (optional)	COST (optional)	NAME AND ADDRESS OR NAME AND LICENSE NO.
1021									
1022									
1023									
1024									
1025									
1026									
1027									
1028									
1029									
1030									
1031									
1032									
1033									
1034									
1035									

DISPOSITION

	SELL PRICE (optional)	DATE	NAME	NICS NUMBER (optional)	ADDRESS OR LICENSE NO. OF LICENSEE, OR FORM 4473 SERIAL NO. IF FORMS 4473 FILED NUMERICALLY
1021					
1022					
1023					
1024					
1025					
1026					
1027					
1028					
1029					
1030					
1031					
1032					
1033					
1034					
1035					